D1144716

Mind-Bending Sports Puzzles

Editor: Colleen Collier
Puzzle Compilers: Philip Carter, Hazel Richardson
Additional Contributors: Christine Pountney, Peter Sorenti
Page layout & Design: Linley Clode
Cover design: Gary Inwood Studios

Published by:
LAGOON BOOKS
PO BOX 311, KT2 5QW, UK
PO Box 990676, Boston, MA 02199, USA

www.lagoongames.com

ISBN 1-902813-51-0

© LAGOON BOOKS, 2001.

Lagoon Books is a trademark of
Lagoon Trading Company Limited.
All rights reserved.

Printed in Singapore.

Mind-Bending
Sports Puzzles

LAGOON
BOOKS

INTRODUCTION

If you are keen on sport and mad about puzzles, here is the ultimate combination of fun just for you!

All the Mind-Bending puzzle books have been carefully compiled to give the reader a refreshingly wide range of challenges, some requiring only a small leap of perception, others deep and detailed thought. All the books share an eye-catching and distinctive style that presents each problem in an appealing and intriguing way. And this one has been compiled especially with the sports enthusiast in mind, as all the clever conundrums and puzzles share a common 'sports' theme.

Every sport you can imagine is mentioned here along with a huge array of puzzles to try and test you. How well will you score? Will you be a sporting hero or merely a perplexed puzzler?

What is the minimum number of cushions the white ball needs to rebound off in order to pot the black ball in pocket A and avoid hitting any of the red balls?

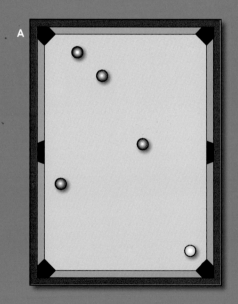

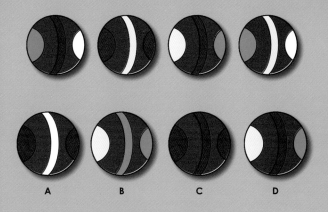

A   B   C   D

Geoff, the superstitious bowler, has used the balls shown in sequence for the last four cricket matches. Which one will he use on Saturday for the next match against Southwicks County Cricket Club?

Bertie Dunn, the lowest scoring player in the Boston Bangles basketball team has been offered a transfer deal. The manager of Seattle Raiders has offered him a 10 per cent cut in his weekly wages followed by an immediate raise of 11 per cent the week after his transfer. Should Bertie take this offer?

Piers Wallace, the manager of Blinthorpe City soccer team is distraught. At half-time, bookings have left him with only seven players. What formation can he use to have three rows of three players while still keeping his goalkeeper and three defending players?

In a race between five cars, the position at five stages of the race is shown. From the options A, B, C, D and E shown, what should the position at the next stage of the race be?

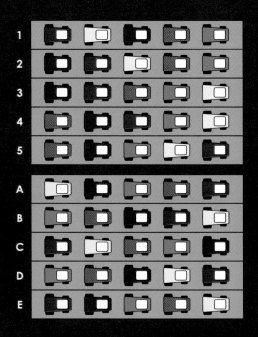

Susan is having a great day out at the races. She has already picked three winners whose numbers were 3, 5, 8, and 13. What number horse should she pick in the next race to continue her winning streak?

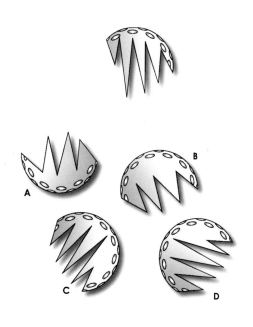

The Golf pro at our local club once hit a golf ball so hard that it completely split in two. One half of the unfortunate ball is shown but which of the others is the matching half?

An epidemic of tennis elbow has resulted in there being only 39 entrants for the Australian Open tennis championship. How many matches need to be played to find the winner?

Which of these balls is the odd one out?

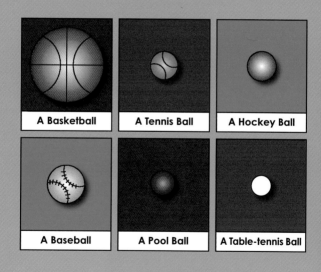

| A Basketball | A Tennis Ball | A Hockey Ball |
| A Baseball | A Pool Ball | A Table-tennis Ball |

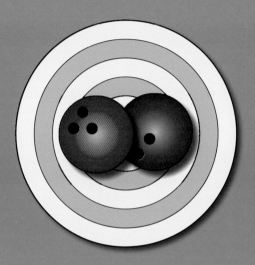

Two players have identical 12lb bowling balls, one red and one blue. The player with the red ball sends his ball down the lane at 15mph and the player with the blue ball sends his at 25mph. Which ball goes through the most number of revolutions?

Two goals are scored in the soccer match between Barchester Rovers and Swindon Town. Swindon Town did not win. What are the chances that Barchester Rovers won the match?

Two-thirds of the way into his race, a cyclist gets a flat and has to carry his bike the rest of the way. It takes him twice as long as it did to ride the first two-thirds, so how many times faster does he ride than walk?

In a practice soccer match lasting 90 minutes, one team of 11 players alternates 4 reserves equally with each player. This means that all players, including reserves, are on the pitch for the same length of time, so how long is each player on the pitch?

I ce hockey is an extremely dangerous game. In the
Alberta Broncos, 70 per cent of players have lost a foot,
75 per cent of players have lost a hand, 80 per cent of
players have lost an eye, and 85 per cent have lost an ear.
What percentage must, at least, have lost all four?

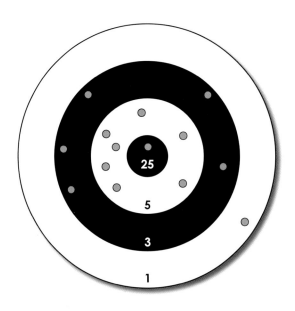

25

5

3

1

Ronald, Bill and George are taking part in an archery contest. So far they have hit the target 14 times between them as indicated. Bill has scored half as many again as Ronald, and George has scored half as many again as Bill. Altogether, they have scored 76. How many has each man scored and what are their individual hits?

On their first ascent of Mount Everest, Al, Bert, and Clive come to a steep and narrow gorge and are dismayed to see their friends David, Eamon, and Fred descending the gorge towards them. As the climbers are guaranteed to fall if they try to climb over more than one man at a time or if they go backwards, can they exchange places without anyone falling or leaving the gorge?

W hat, logically, should be the number of the winning horse?

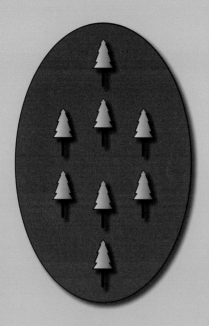

In training, Norse Winderbottom, the famous cross -country skier, is asked by his coach to ski around every marked tree in the forest without stopping and without crossing his path. How can Norse do this?

	MEN	WOMEN
Mens' singles	23	
Ladies' singles		17
Mens' doubles	13 pairs	
Ladies' doubles		9 pairs
Mixed doubles	14 pairs	

At the local tennis club, the following members entered the Annual Knockout Championships for singles and doubles. As they were all knockout competitions, the members had to be reduced first to 16-8-4-2 by using byes. No one forfeited out of the competitions, therefore all the matches were played. So how many matches had been played before the five tournament winners were decided?

Wendy Sitight and her horse Noddy faced a difficult challenge at their previous horse-jumping competition. They had to jump over all nine fences, but Wendy was only allowed to turn her horse three times. How did she do it?

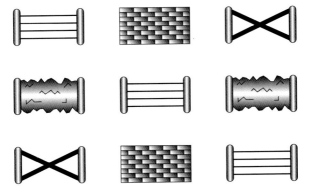

Which of these colorful soccer balls is the odd one out?

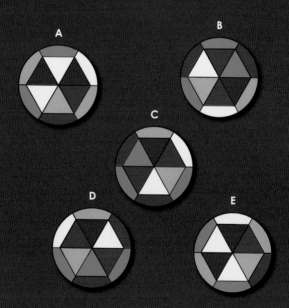

The New York Yippees football team has two extraordinary players. They are both six feet, nine inches tall. What is even stranger is that they share the same surname, the same mother, and were even born on the same day. But they are not twins. How is this possible?

In the final lap of the Canadian Grand Prix, just ten cars are left in the race, the leader being car number seven, followed by car number four. Bringing up the rear is car number twelve. What, logically, should be the number of the car second from last?

Which number comes next in this sporting sequence?

20
18
13
10

Bill, George and Jimmy are having a game of darts. After each had thrown three times, the following are the nine scores registered (starting with the largest amount through to the smallest amount). Bill won twice as much as George, so what was the total score of each man for his three throws?

65 52 47 39 26 23 21 15 12

In a lacrosse game, Susan caught the ball two-thirds as many times as her friend Clare would have caught the ball, if Clare had caught it six times more than half as many as Susan would have caught it, if Susan had caught it three times less than Annabel would have caught it. How many times, therefore, did Susan catch the ball?

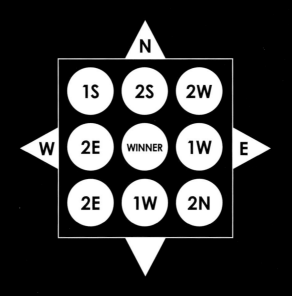

The rifle club has devised a new style of competition for its Annual Championship whereby each competitor is given the same target. The nine circles have to be hit in the correct order by following the compass directions on each. The last circle is marked winner, so in addition to being the top sharpshooter, the contestants have to work out which circle to hit first. What is the first circle?

Despite the fine June weather, the cricket match between England and the West Indies at the Oval has dragged on into the early evening. Steven Wilkins is next to bat and needs a 'four' to win the match. He is facing the West Indies' finest spinbowler and notices that one of the fielders to his left seems to have hurt his arm and that there is a mild northerly wind. Where should Steven direct his shot to have the best chance of winning the match?

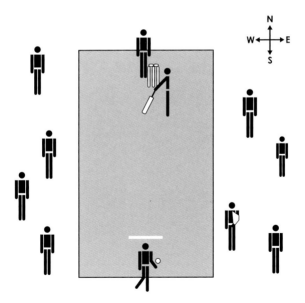

After a dreadful start to the season, our local soccer team succeeded in their tenth match of the season with a great high-scoring victory. The captain, who was something of a mathematician, suddenly noticed something rather unusual.

"I have just written down our first ten scores in the order of matches played and have noticed the following…

"The first score is the number of times we scored 1

"The second score is the number of times we scored 2

"The third score is the number of times we scored 3

"The fourth score is the number of times we scored 4

"and it carries on like this right up to our tenth score, which is the number of times we scored zero".

What were the ten scores in the first ten matches?

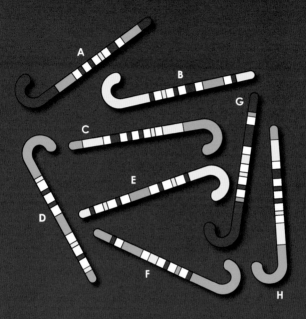

Which one of these hockey sticks is the odd one out?

Niles Longlegg, the famous long-distance runner, is in training. His coach has marked out a grid and asked him to run around every square in it. How many squares will Niles have to run around in total?

At the end of the basketball season, the team's four leading scorers had amassed a total of 594 points, the leading scorer exceeding his next three highest scoring opponents by 76 points, 142 points and 164 points respectively. What was the total score for each of the four players?

The shirts for the rugby teams of the neighboring countries of Bangaloon and Reedland are designed to relate to their flags. Below are the flag and rugby shirt for Bangaloon. If this is the Reedland flag, which rugby shirt do they use for their national team?

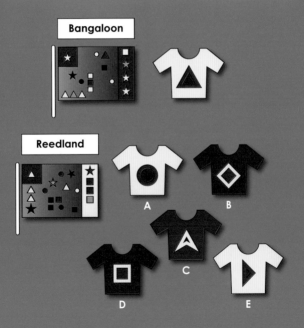

Bangaloon

Reedland

A

B

C

D

E

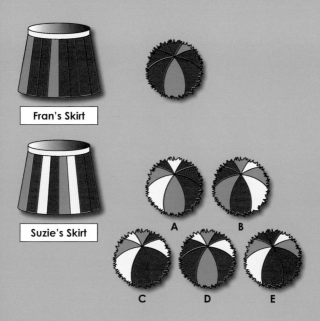

Fran's Skirt

Suzie's Skirt

A

B

C

D

E

This is Fran the cheerleader's skirt and her matching pom pom. If Suzie's skirt looks like this, which one is her pom pom?

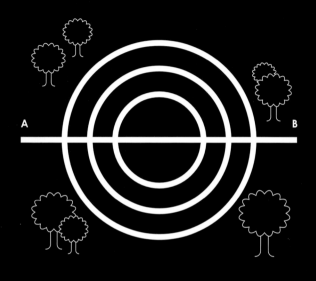

A boxer takes the same training run every week, and runs from point A to point B while traveling every part of the route shown. Can you complete his route without taking your finger from the paper? Lines may cross but must not be retraced.

Rain had stopped play at Wimbledon yet again and two partners in the doubles were trying to amuse themselves by setting each other puzzles. *"Here's one for you,"* said Pat, *"just four of these five pieces can be fitted together in the shape of a tennis ball"*. Which four pieces will solve the puzzle?

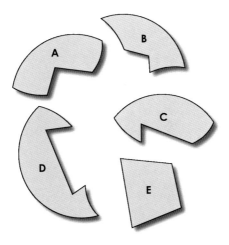

On a racecard (which shows the position each horse finished in the previous seven races), the form for each runner is shown. However, the form for Runner Five has been omited. Can you figure out what its form should be from the other four horses shown?

THE ENIGMA STAKES – 2.30PM
FOR THREE-YEAR-OLD FILLIES

RUNNER	NAME	FORM
1	Tralala	3516924
2	Ladybird	6924351
3	Contessa	4351692
4	Skylark	1692435
5	Huntress	?

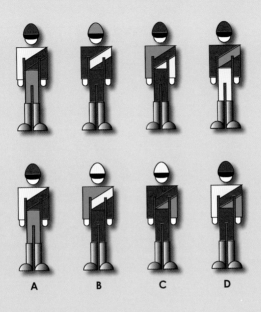

Hilary Blanchett owns five racehorses. Four of her jockeys' colors are shown, but what colors does the fifth jockey wear?

A B C D

Two cricket batsmen are making a high-scoring stand. The score of one batsman is the same as the other if the digits of his score are reversed. In the last over, both batsmen scored one run but prior to that, one batsman's score had been twice that of his partner. How many runs has each batsman scored?

Footballer Shane Riggers is not playing at his best. As you can see, each time he receives the ball, he runs a shorter distance before being brought down by a Boston Matches player. How far will he be able to run the next time he receives the ball?

CATCH	DISTANCE RUN
1	10m
2	7 m
3	4.9m
4	3.43m
5	2.49m
6	?

W hich swimmer is two places behind the swimmer who is three places in front of the swimmer who is five places behind the swimmer who is one place in front of the swimmer who is two places behind the swimmer in the blue costume?

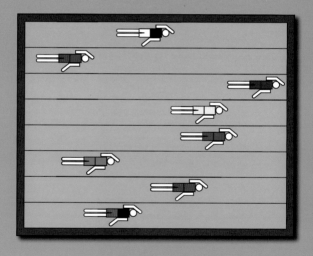

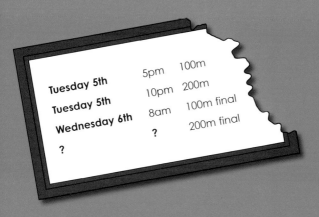

Tuesday 5th   5pm   100m

Tuesday 5th   10pm   200m

Wednesday 6th   8am   100m final

?   ?   200m final

Representing his country at the Olympics, sprinter Bert Speedy has just been given these dates and starting times for his first three races. What date and time will the final of the 200m be held?

" I had quite a catch the other day," said Peter, "A prize pike". "How much did it weigh?" asked a very doubtful-sounding Thomas. "450 lbs divided by half its own weight," boasted Peter. How much then did the pike allegedly weigh?

Here is a photograph of the Clacton Rovers soccer team. Which player is two players to the left of the player who is two players to the right of the player who is three players to the right of the player who is two players to the left of the player immediately to the right of player number six?

W hen the above is folded to form a cube, which is the only one of the following that can be produced?

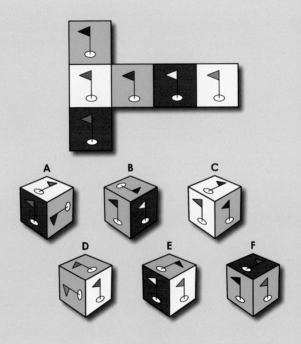

A

B

C

D

E

F

In a darts competition, each dart scores either 40, 39, 24, 23, 17 or 16 points. How many darts must therefore be thrown to score exactly 100 points?

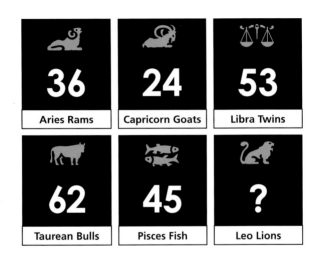

36 Aries Rams	**24** Capricorn Goats	**53** Libra Twins
62 Taurean Bulls	**45** Pisces Fish	**?** Leo Lions

The final scores were announced on the first Sunday of a new Football League. How many did the Leo Lions score?

Rory, Roger and Roy each scored points seven times in the rugby match against Kiwi Island. Rory scored with twice as many drop kicks as Roger and fewer tries than Roy. Roy made half as many tries as Roger did, so how many times did Roy score with a drop kick?

A man jogs at six miles per hour over a certain route, but then runs out of steam completely and has to walk back over the same route at four miles per hour. What is his average speed for the total journey?

Four of the five yachts that finished the race have something in common, but which is the odd one out?

Fred Snailfoot has decided to run in this year's New York marathon. For his target finish time, he needs to run at an average speed of 9 miles per hour. Halfway through the race, his coach tells him that he has only been running at 4.5 miles per hour. How fast will Fred have to run to finish the race in his target time?

Four ice-skaters spin in circles a third of a mile long. They start in the center at the same time and then travel at 6, 9, 12 and 15 mph. In 20 minutes, how many times will they have simultaneously returned to the spots from where they started?

Of the leading scorers in the current baseball season, Alan has scored more points than Bill and Colin, Colin has scored more than Dave, Edward has scored less than Bill but more than Dave, Alan has scored less than Fred, and Colin has scored more than Edward. Can you list the six men from highest score to lowest?

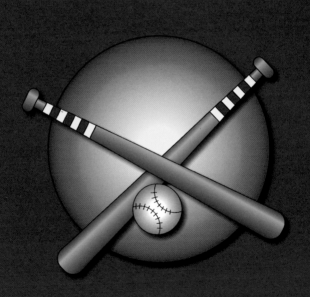

The French soccer team is made up of players from many other teams. There are at least two players in the team who have exactly the same number of team-mates present. Is this possible?

Two men run a race of 200 meters that Carl wins by 20 meters. Because of this, they decide to make things fairer for the next race by making Carl stand 20 meters behind the line, thereby giving Pete a 20 meter headstart. They both run the second race at exactly the same speed as before. What is the result?

At a photo shoot, ten members of the Winstanly netball team line up in a triangular formation. The team photographer wants to rearrange the girls so that the formation points the other way. How many girls will have to move?

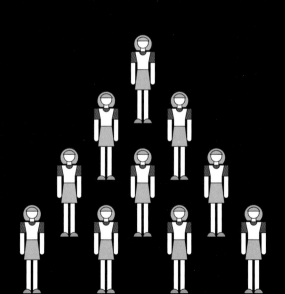

The game of croquet is played with six hoops and a central peg on a lawn 35 yards long and 28 yards wide. Four balls are used, which are colored blue, red, black and yellow. Can you arrange these four balls and one of the hoops in each line of the grid below so that no two of the same colored balls and no two hoops are in any horizontal, vertical or diagonal line?

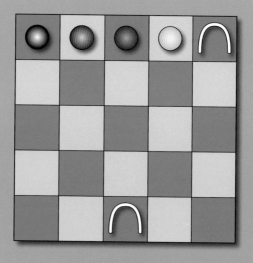

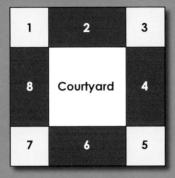

Eight shot-putters visit Rome to take part in a competition. They stay in a lovely hotel that has eight rooms around a central courtyard. Being a lover of symmetry, the manager decides to allocate the rooms so that there are four shot-putters on all four sides of the courtyard. How does he do this?

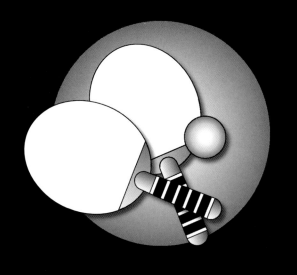

Our local newspaper organized a table-tennis tournament. Anyone who entered had to win two games in a row to win a prize and each player had to play just three games altogether, alternating between a strong player and a weak player. What are the best tactics to employ in this situation? Is it best to play 'Strong – Weak – Strong' or 'Weak – Strong – Weak'?

A team of rowers row two kilometers downstream in two minutes. When they are rowing upstream, they take four minutes to row two kilometers. How long would it take them to row two kilometers in a lake?

"*That's amazing,*" said one of the spectators at the Marathon. "*Look at the numbers on the runners' shirts*". "*What about it?*" said one of his friends. "*Can't you see the sequence?*" said his friend. "*I can,*" chimed up another spectator, "*I see what you are getting at*". What number should replace the question mark?

Brian Baffle wants to buy a player from Steven Slimeball, the manager of Poolton Wanderers. Mr Slimeball says that Brian can have the player for one million dollars plus half his price. How much should Brian offer?

Recently I chaired a noisy meeting at our Squash club in which we all disagreed so strongly that several of the committee walked out. I remarked that if I had also walked out, then only one-third of the original number would have been left. *"Yes,"* said one of my colleagues, *"but if Susan and Tony had stayed, we would have only lost half the original number"*. How many members were present at the start of the meeting?

Three basketball players had a heavy drinking session after winning a game and fell asleep at a friend's house. When they awoke, they started laughing when they realized that someone had shaved off their team-mates eyebrows. One of them quickly stopped laughing, realizing that he had also had his eyebrows shaved off. How did he know without feeling his face or looking in a mirror?

In the Annual World Team Golf Championships, six teams – Japan, England, USA, Australia, South Africa and Scotland – are battling it out at the top of the leader board. This was the position at the half-way stage. How many under par is each team?

USA is one more under par than Australia

South Africa is one more under par than USA

Japan is one more under par than South Africa

Scotland is one more under par than Japan

England is one more under par than Scotland and is twice as many under par as Australia

There are rumors of match fixing in a cricket tournament. There are eight cricket balls supplied for the next match and the umpire thinks that one of them might be weighted. But the match is due to begin any moment. With a set of balancing scales, how can he find the weighted ball in just two weighings?

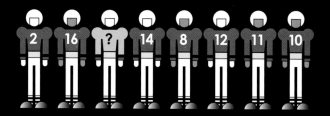

At the Superbowl final, eight team members are lined up waiting to take the field. What number is missing from the jersey of the third player from the left?

Will Tuffguy, the world champion weightlifter, has been challenged by his main rival, Beefy Brawn, to a weightlifting duel. Beefy asks Will if he will lift an unknown weight and if he accepts and doesn't succeed, he must surrender his title. Being a good sport, Beefy gives Will a few clues but how much does the unknown weight actually weigh?

There are a number of cars competing in the Millennium Rally Cross. Which of their numberplates is the odd one out?

92 BAR S

64 TOK J

76 MON C

98 NAG J

56 MEL A

Peter Pippin enters an archery competition where he has to hit one of several targets. The odd one out carries the highest score so which one should he aim for?

As the first seven horses crossed the finishing line, Ben was half a length behind Baby Face, and Consort was half a length in front of Heatherset. Heatherset was in front of Ben, and Candida had more than three horses behind her. Piperton finished a length in front of Heatherset and Speedwell finished half a length in front of Candida. There was at least half a length between each two horses. What was the order of the finish?

A cricket batsman is out for 35 runs, which raises his batting average for the season from 15 to 17. How many runs would he have had to score to bring his average to 19?

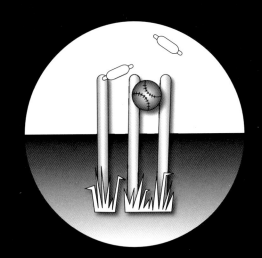

Ronald, Bill and George are taking part in a shooting match and so far they have hit the target 17 times between them as indicated. George has scored a third as many again as Bill, and Bill has scored a third as many again as Ronald. Altogether they have scored 111, so how many has each man scored and what are their individual hits?

25

5

3

1

At the start of the Grand National horserace, I correctly counted the number of legs of the horses plus the jockeys, and the total came to 216. How many runners were in the race?

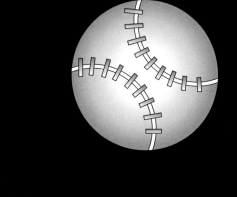

In this year's Baseball league, Frankie the Slammer has scored three more home runs than Colin the Crasher. However, if Colin had three times as many home runs as he has now, he would have three more home runs than the combined number of home runs they have now. How many home runs has Frankie made?

In each container are a number of tennis balls. Logically, how many tennis balls should be in the container with the question mark?

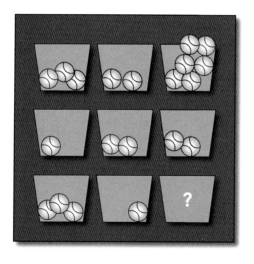

In a game of basketball, the net is mounted five feet above the floor plus half its own height. Therefore, how high is the net mounted above the floor?

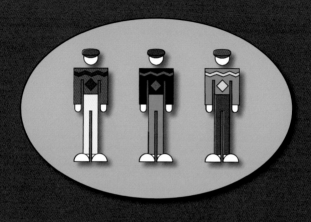

Three men, Mr Green, Mr Black and Mr Brown were playing a round of golf together. Half-way through the game, Mr Green remarked that although he had realized that all their names were colors, he had only just realized that they were wearing green, black and brown sweaters as well. *"Yes,"* said one of the others, *"I'd already noticed that, but none of us is wearing the same colored sweater as our own name. For example, I am wearing a brown sweater".* Which color sweater was each wearing?

Three ex-England cricket captains were discussing their scores. Lenny said, *"I scored 9 – I scored 2 fewer than Teddy and 1 more than Alec"*. Teddy said, *"I did not score the lowest – the difference between my score and Alec's was 3 and Alec scored 12"*. Alec then said, *"I scored fewer runs than Lenny and Lenny scored 10. Teddy did score 3 more than Lenny though"*. If each man made one incorrect statement out of the three, what were their scores?

After a game of soccer, three brothers arrived home, one of them having been red-carded, but they did not want to admit to their father which one. Each of the sons made just one statement to their father, the only information other than this being that at least one of the statements was true and at least one was false. From this information, was it possible for their father to work out which of his sons had been red-carded?

Danny said, *"Tommy was not red-carded"*.

Tommy said, *"I was not red-carded"*.

Pete said, *"I was red-carded"*.

SOLUTIONS

Page 6

Three cushions.

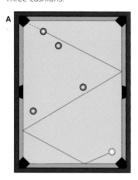

Page 7

The answer is C, because the middle stripe alternates blue/yellow, the left-hand mark alternates green/blue/yellow, and the right-hand mark alternates white/blue/green.

Page 8

No. If, for example, Bertie is earning $1000 per week before the transfer, a cut of 10 per cent will reduce his earnings to $900. A raise of 11 per cent will only increase his wages to $999 (11 per cent of 900), leaving him worse off.

Page 9

Page 10

The answer is D, because at each stage the middle car only changes its position in the order. At stage one it drops to last, then the middle car moves to first, and they continue alternating first/last in this way.

Page 11

Number 22 – the numbers follow a pattern of the previous number doubled with an ascending number subtracted. The next horse is 13 x 2 – 4 = 22.

Page 12

The answer is C.

Page 13

A total of 38. Knockout matches always operate to the power of two. There need to be seven initial matches to remove seven players,

followed by 16 matches, then
eight, then four, then two, then
the final match.

Page 14

A basketball because it is the only
ball which is propeled with the
hands and not an implement.

Page 15

Both go through exactly the same
number of revolutions because,
although at different speeds, they
cover the same distance.

Page 16

If we know that Swindon Town
did not win, then the chances of
Barchester Rovers winning the
match are 2 out of 5 (taking the
possibility of own goals into
account).

Page 17

Four times faster. He walks one-
third of the way – which is half as
far as he rides – in twice the time.

Page 18

66 minutes, because (90 x 11) ÷
15 = 66.

Page 19

30 per cent have got both feet.
25 per cent have got both hands.
20 per cent of players have got

both eyes. 15 per cent have got
both ears. So 90 per cent at most
have both of something, leaving
10 per cent at least who have lost
all four!

Page 20

Ronald has scored 16 (2 x 5) +
(2 x 3); Bill has scored 24 (3 x 5) +
(3 x 3); and George has scored 36
(1 x 25) + (2 x 5) + (1 x 1).

Page 21

If Al, Bert, and Clive are labeled as
A B C, and David, Eamon, and
Fred are labeled as D E F, this is the
sequence they should climb to get
past each other safely.

FED ABC
FEA DBC
FEA BDC
FAE BDC
AFE BDC
AFB EDC
AFB ECD
AFB CED
ABF CED
ABC FED

Page 22

It should be 21, if you add the
sequence of odd numbers 1,3,5,7
at each stage.

SOLUTIONS

Page 23

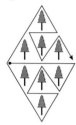

Page 24

In each event there must be just one winner, therefore there must be the same number of matches as the remainder in each tournament to produce the required number of losers. The number of matches played has to be 22 + 16 + 12 + 8 + 13 = 71 matches.

Page 25

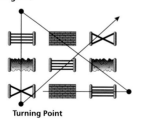

Turning Point

Page 26

The answer is D, because A is the same as E, and B is the same as C, but D has no equivalent.

Page 27

They are two out of three triplets.

Page 28

Number three, because the sum of the number of each pair of cars is one more than the sum of the numbers of the previous pair.

Page 29

They are alternate clockwise numbers on a dartboard, so the next number will be 2.

Page 30

Bill scored 26 + 39 + 47 = 112; George scored 12 + 23 + 21 = 56; and Jimmy scored 15 + 52 + 65 = 132.

Page 31

Six times.

Page 32

The first circle that needs to be hit is the one marked 2S.

Page 33

The fielders in this position are more likely to be affected by the glare of the setting sun and by the long shadows cast by other players.

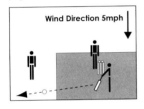

Page 34

2 1 0 0 0 1 0 0 0 6

Page 35

The answer is F. The pattern of stripes on the sticks does not matter, as it is the orientation of the stick that is different.

Page 36

30 (1 + 4 + 9 + 16).

Page 37

Add 594 + 76 + 142 + 164 = 976 and then divide by 4 = 244. 244 is therefore the score of the highest scorer. The next highest is 168, the

next 102, and finally 80.

Page 38

The answer is B, as the pattern for the shirts comes from the shape left after all the circles on the flags are joined together.

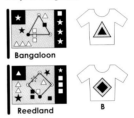

Page 39

The sequence of colors on the skirt from right to left runs clockwise around the pom pom, so the answer is D.

Page 40

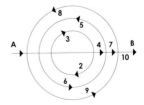

SOLUTIONS

Page 41

Page 42

Each set of numbers is the last four numbers of the previous set, followed by the first three, so the answer is 2435169.

Page 43

The answer is C, as the color sequence 'red, yellow, blue, red, and green' cycles downward through hat, top, sash, top and trousers.

Page 44

73 and 37.

Page 45

1.68m.

Page 46

The swimmer in the green costume.

Page 47

Wednesday 6th at 4pm. For each race, take the time of the previous race and add the number of hours shown to that time to find out the time of the next race.

Page 48

30 lbs (450 divided by 15 = 30).

Page 49

Player four.

Page 50

The answer is B.

Page 51

Six.

Page 52

The numbers 3, 6, 2, 4, and 5 are being repeated in the same order, so the answer is 36.

Page 53

Rory – six drop kicks and one try
Roger – three drop kicks and four tries
Roy – five drop kicks and two tries.

Page 54

4.8 mph, because if, say, the journey is 6 miles each way, then at 6 mph the outward jog would take 1 hour and the inward walk 1.5 hours. This means that it takes 2.5 hours to travel 12 miles, or 1 hour to travel 4.8 miles.

Page 55

The answer is 3, because 1 and 4 have the same colors reversed, as have 2 and 5.

Page 56

It isn't possible for Fred to do it, as he has already taken up his target time getting half-way around the course.

Page 57

In 20 minutes, they travel one-third of a mile 6, 9, 12 and 15 times. The largest number these numbers are all divisible by is three, so the answer is three times.

Page 58

Fred, Alan, Bill, Colin, Edward, then Dave.

Page 59

Yes. If each player is given a label denoting the number of team-mates present, the label can only be one of ten numbers (0 and 11 cannot both appear). So one number must appear twice.

Page 60

Carl still wins again! We know from the first race that Carl runs 200 meters at the same time that Pete runs 180 meters. It follows,

therefore, that as Carl starts 20 meters behind the line, the men will be dead level at 20 meters short of the winning line. And as Carl is the faster runner, he goes on to overtake Pete in the last 20 meters to win the race.

Page 61

The answer is three.

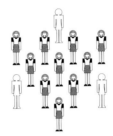

Page 62

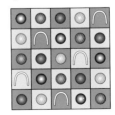

SOLUTIONS

Page 63

He puts two shot-putters in each corner room.

Page 64

'Strong – Weak – Strong'. To win a prize you must win once against the strong player and this arrangement gives you two chances, assuming you beat the weak player.

Page 65

Two minutes, 40 seconds. Rowing upstream against the current slows the rowers to half a kilometer per minute and they can row at one kilometer per minute with the current. So the current makes a 15-second difference and the rowers' speed is three-quarters of a kilometer per minute. The two-kilometer journey in slack water therefore takes two and two-third minutes.

Page 66

715, because starting with the first runner and ignoring boundaries, the sequence of odd numbers appears as 21, 19, 17, 15, 13, 11, 9, 7, 5, 3, 1.

Page 67

Two million dollars.

Page 68

18 were originally present at the meeting. It had to be an even number, also divisible by 3. Trying 6 or 12 won't give the correct figure so try 18. Then, 11 walked out, leaving 7. If I had gone, only 6 (one-third) would have been left. If Susan and Tony had stayed, then 9 (half) would have remained.

Page 69

He could see that the other two players had their eyebrows shaved off also and that they were laughing at him, so it was a simple deduction to work out that he too had had his eyebrows shaved off.

Page 70

Australia	5 under
USA	6 under
South Africa	7 under
Japan	8 under
Scotland	9 under
England	10 under

Page 71

He divides the eight balls into two groups of three, and a group of two. He weighs the two groups of three against each other. If one group is heavier than the other, it must contain the weighted ball. He picks the heavier group and weighs two of the balls against each other. If one is heavier than the other, it must be the weighted ball. If both balls weigh the same, the unweighed ball is the weighted ball. If both groups of three balls weigh the same, then the weighted ball must be in the group of two. He then weighs the two balls to find the weighted ball.

Page 72
5, as there are two alternate sequences – 2, 5, 8, 11 and 16, 14, 12, 10.

Page 73
The unknown weight is 600 kg.

Page 74
98 NAG J is the odd one out. Each license plate represents the year, followed by the first three letters of the city, followed by the first letter of the country, of twentieth-century Olympic games venues. 98 NAG J is the odd one out because it was a Winter Olympics, whereas the others were Summer Games.

92 Barcelona Spain

64 Tokyo Japan

76 Montreal Canada

98 Nagano Japan

56 Melbourne Australia

Page 75
The odd target is the star-shaped one as it is the only one that is not the same when turned 180 degrees.

Page 76
Speedwell, Candida, Piperton, Consort, Heatherset, Baby Face, and then Ben.

Page 77
The answer is 55. Score 135 for 9 innings = average 15; score 170 for 10 innings = average 17; score 190 for 10 innings = average 19.

SOLUTIONS

Page 78

Ronald has scored 27 (5 x 5) +
(2 x 1); Bill has scored 36 (1 x 25)
+ (2 x 5) + (1 x 1); and George has
scored 48 (1 x 25) + (1 x 3) +
(4 x 5).

Page 79

36 runners as 36 horses x 4 legs =
144 and 36 jockeys x 2 legs = 72.

Page 80

Frankie has 9 and Colin has 6 (x 3
= 18).

Page 81

Multiply the first two containers
together to get the number in the
third container, and then looking
down, divide the first by the
second to obtain the number in
the third container. The answer is
three.

Page 82

Ten feet.

Page 83

Mr Green must be wearing black
because the man who spoke last is
wearing brown, and he is not
wearing green. Therefore, the
others must be Mr Black wearing
brown and Mr Brown wearing
green.

Page 84

Lenny scored 10, Teddy scored 12,
and Alec scored 9.

Page 85

It was Danny who was red-carded.
If it had been Tommy, all
statements would be false, and if
it had been Pete, all statements
would be true.

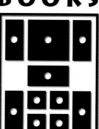